CONTENTS

DEVELOPING IDEAS

EVALUATION

HELP!

The Shopping Basket

CREDITS
Published by Scholastic Ltd,
Villiers House,
Clarendon Avenue,
Leamington Spa,
Warwickshire CV32 5PR
Text © Hilary Braund and Deborah Campbell
© 1999 Scholastic Ltd
   2 3 4 5 6 7 8 9 0   9 0 1 2 3 4 5 6

Author Hilary Braund and Deborah Campbell
Editor Steven Carruthers
Series designer Lynne Joesbury
Designer Clare Brewer
Illustrations redrawn by Clare Brewer from
originals by John Burningham
Cover illustration John Burningham

Designed using Adobe Pagemaker

British Library Cataloguing-in-Publication Data
A catalogue record for this book is available from
the British Library.

ISBN 0-590-53982-5

ACKNOWLEDGEMENTS
Random House Children's Books for the
photograph of John Burningham and the use of
text, front cover and adapted illustrations from
The Shopping Basket by John Burningham
© 1980, John Burningham (1980, Jonathan
Cape Ltd).
Caroline Ewen for other illustrations.

The Shopping Basket

by John Burningham

What's the plot of the story?

Steven's mum sends him on an errand to fetch some shopping from the local shop. On the way back home Steven encounters a range of bullying animals who demand items from his shopping basket. Steven shows that brains are mightier than brawn by outwitting every one of them. But will Steven's mother believe his story?

What's so good about this book?

Although the story line is on the surface fairly simple and repetitive the text is quite challenging for early readers. The book follows the classic John Burningham formula where the distinctions between reality and fantasy are ambivalent. Children will enjoy the humour in the illustrations, and the insults and threats bandied about between Steven and the animals.

About John Burningham

John Burningham wrote and illustrated his first book, *Borka*, in 1963. He started off as an illustrator but nobody would give him a book to illustrate so he decided to write his own. That very first book won a medal.

For over thirty years John Burningham has been writing and illustrating books for children. He is married to Helen Oxenbury. She too is an illustrator of children's books. They have two daughters and one son and they live in London.

Introducing the book

Learning intentions
● to think about how the cover and title of a book draw the reader into the story
● to build awareness of authorship

Organization
● whole class

Look at the front cover of the book with the children. Ask them to read the title. Do they recognise the author's name? Do they know any other stories by John Burningham? Why is the story called 'The Shopping Basket'? Does the little boy in the picture look happy to be out shopping? Do they enjoy going shopping? Where do they think the story is set - in the town or the country? What do they notice about the surroundings?
  Turn to the back cover. What information is given on the back?
  Point out aspects of the book, including the publisher's logo, the bar code and the price. Read the blurb on the back cover. Are there any John Burningham books that they hadn't heard of before? How many of John Burningham's other stories do they have in the classroom?

Reading the story

Learning intentions

● to gain familiarity with the events of the story
● to predict what may happen next
● to discuss reasons for, or causes of, incidents in the story

Organization

● whole class

Start reading the story to the children. After reading the first page ask: What sort of shop will Steven need to go to?

Read up to 'But when he came out of the shop there

was a bear.' *What do you think a bear was doing outside the shop?*

Read up to ' "Me slow!" said the bear.' *What do you think happens when the bear tries to catch the egg?*

Read on until Steven meets the goat. *What do you think the goat will want from Steven's basket?*

Read up to 'there was his mother.' *What do you think Steven's mother will say when she finds some of the shopping is missing?*

Finish reading the story. *What do you think Steven will tell his mother about his shopping trip? Do you think she will believe him?*

Steven's route

Learning intentions
● to recall events from the story in sequence
● to create maps to record sequences of events

Organization
● small group
● photocopiable page 7 – individual copies and one laminated copy

Before starting, photocopy page 7 onto card, cut out and laminate. Add magnetic tape or Blu-Tack to the back of the pictures and labels to enable them to be displayed on a magnetic board or large sheet of paper.

On a magnetic board or large sheet of paper draw a map showing Steven's route from home to the shop. Ask the children to remember all the places Steven passed on his way and the order in which he passed them. Invite the children to add the pictures and labels to the route drawn to create a map of Steven's journey.

Extension
Allow the children to create their own maps of Steven's journey. They may like to draw their own pictures showing the places he passed or, alternatively, you could photocopy page 7 and let the children cut out and stick the pictures onto maps they have drawn. They could label the places in a similar way, either by doing their own writing or by sticking on the photocopied labels.

Story Structure

Learning intentions
● to identify aspects of story structure

Organization
● small group
● copies of photocopiable page 8

On a large sheet of paper write out the three headings as given on photocopiable page 8, ie, *Characters, Settings for events, Items.* Discuss the meaning of these headings with the children. Ask if they can think of one example from the story to fit under each heading.

Give out copies of photocopiable page 8. Read through all the words given at the bottom of the page. Ask the children to work individually or in pairs to write the words under the appropriate headings.

Characters	Settings for events	Items
bear	full litter basket	eggs
goat	shop	oranges

Steven's route

the full litter basket	the men digging up the pavement	the gap in the railings
the house where the nasty dog lived	number 25	the shop

Story structure

Characters	Settings for events	Items

Steven   gap in the railings   eggs

crisps

mother   full litter basket

kangaroo

doughnuts   bear   apples

elephant

house where the nast lived

basket   shop

note

oranges

number 25   monkey   bananas

goat

men digging up the pavement   pig

What happened next?

Learning intentions
● to use illustrations as an impetus for writing
● to use the style of the story to structure the children's own writing

Organization
● small group
● multiple copies of the book

For this activity children in pairs will need access to a copy of the book. Ask the children to turn to the page where Steven is confronted by the bear. Read through the text together. Ask the children if they know what '. . .' indicates at the end of the text. Explain that the story continues over the page but that the story is told in the illustrations and not in the text. Invite the children to tell you what happens in the picture in their own words. Act as scribe to create some shared writing as if John Burningham had written the story to go with the picture.

Divide the children into pairs and give each pair a sheet of paper. Working together they should select one of the other pictures that has no text and share the writing to create an addition to the story as before. They should read the text immediately before and after the picture along with their own writing to ensure it makes sense.

Extension
You could create an extended version of 'The Shopping Basket' by writing out the whole story, including the children's contributions, either by hand or using a word processor.

Story connections

Learning intentions
● to locate key words in the text
● to use mapping to represent relationships between features of the story structure

Organization
● small group
● copies of photocopiable page 10
● copies of the book

Ask the children to take one of the animals and ask them if they can remember what food the animal wanted, what threat they made to Steven, and what Steven accused them of being, eg *kangaroo, apples, thump him* and *clumsy*. Write these words on a board or flip chart. Look at the relevant page together and invite the children to show you where the words appear to see if they were correct.

Give out copies of photocopiable page 10. Explain that the children should choose one colour pencil for each animal and draw lines to match the animals to the relevant three words. They should use a copy of the book to help them.

Story connections

Animal	Food	Threat	Insult
kangaroo	bananas	hug	slow
pig	crisps	thump	noisy
elephant	apples	pull	fat
goat	doughnuts	squash	stupid
bear	eggs	whack	short
monkey	oranges	butt	clumsy

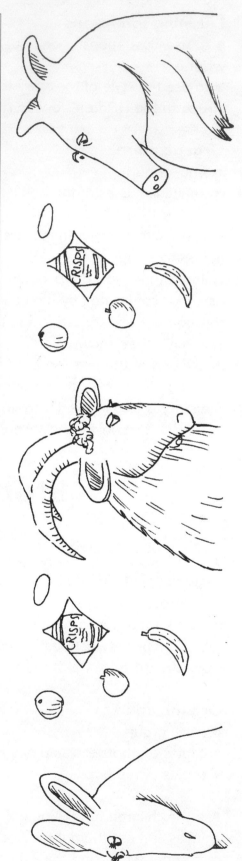

What did Steven buy?

Learning intentions
● to hear and identify initial sounds in words

Organization
● whole class

Recap on the items that Steven bought at the shop. Write Steven's shopping list on a large sheet of paper, omitting the initial letter of each word. Invite the children to tell you which letters are missing. Ask them to think of other things that Steven could have bought at the shop. Invite the children one at a time to come up to the board and write the initial letter of the item they are thinking of. The rest of the class have three guesses to find out what the item is using the initial letter as a clue. When they have guessed or been told what the item is the teacher or child should write the complete word on the board to add to the shopping list.

Give Me That!

Learning intentions
● to recall events from the story
● to locate key words in the text
● to match text to pictures

Organization
● small group
● copies of photocopiable pages 12 and 13
● a 6-page zig-zag book for each child

Ask the children to recall all the animals that were in the story. Can they remember which item of Steven's shopping each animal wanted? Use the book to help them remember.

Show them photocopiable pages 12 and 13 and read through the text contained in the speech bubbles together. Explain to the children that they are to cut out the animals and stick one on each page of a six-page zig-zag book. They should then try to find the correct speech bubble to cut out and stick with each animal. The pages could be completed by adding a picture of the appropriate food item. Ask the children to read their finished books back to you.

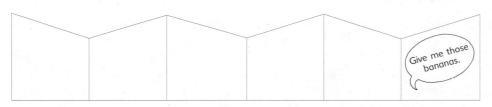

Give me those bananas.

Give me that! I

Give me those bananas.

I want those eggs.

Give me those crisps.

Give me the oranges you have in your basket.

Give me those apples you have in your basket.

Give me those doughnuts.

Give me that! 2

Shopping basket game

Learning intentions
● to read on sight a number of familiar words from the text
● to hear and identify initial sounds in words

Organization
● small group
● copies of photocopiable page 15 enlarged and laminated
● copies of photocopiable page 16 cut out and laminated
● dice

Enlarge photocopiable page 15 and copy it onto card. Ensure there are enough for each child in the group to have one each. Photocopy a similar number of copies of page 16, cutting out the pictures.

Laminate the shopping baskets and the cut out food items.

Explain to the children that they are going to play a game to collect all the items that Steven had in his shopping basket. Give each child a photocopied shopping basket and place all the food pictures in the centre of the table. Each child takes it in turns to throw a dice. They should collect the item relating to the number they have thrown on the dice, ie, *1 = packet of crisps, 2 = doughnuts, etc.* The picture should be placed on the basket next to the corresponding word. Encourage the children to use their knowledge of initial sounds to identify the words on their baskets. The winner is the first to collect all six items and match them correctly.

Sentence Building

Learning intentions
● to order words within a sentence
● to substitute and extend patterns in reading through introducing new words

Organization
● whole class

Reread the story to the class encouraging the children to join in with the repeated phrase 'And/So Steven hurried on home carrying his basket.' Write out the two different versions of the sentence – ie, *beginning 'And/So'* – on a large sheet of paper and ask the children how they are the same or different. Cut a strip of card into separate word cards showing the words from the repeated phrase. Using magnetic tape or Blu-Tack to fix the words to the board, invite the children to put the words into the right order.

Use the repeated phrase as an opportunity for shared writing based on a frame sentence. For early stage readers the sentence could be changed by substituting the names of children in the class and other items they may be carrying home, eg, *And Martha hurried on home carrying her violin.*

Shopping basket game (basket)

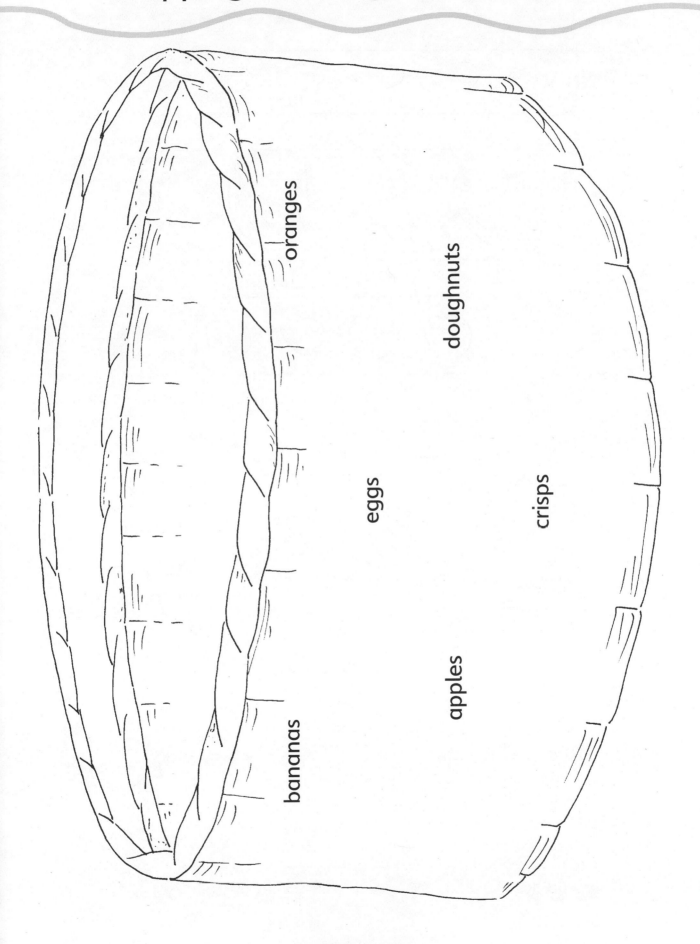

Shopping basket game (food)

The animals speak

Learning intentions
● to use alternative words and phrases to enhance meaning

Organization
● small group
● copies of photocopiable page 18

Recap with the children the whole class activity 'Sentence Building' in which the meaning of a sentence was changed by substituting one word for another. Look in the book at how each animal asks Steven for an item of food and notice how John Burningham uses 'said' throughout the story. Ask the children if they can suggest any words that can be used instead of 'said'. Write all their suggestions on the board or a large sheet of paper. Ask if any of them would be inappropriate in the context of the story and cross these out, eg, *whispered, asked*. Help the children to add any other words to the list that may be appropriate to the animals in the story, eg, *growled, grunted, chattered*.

Write on the board ' "I want those eggs," _____ the bear.' and ask the children to select one of their suggested words as an alternative to 'said' in order to complete the sentence, eg, *growled, shouted, roared*.

Give out copies of photocopiable page 18 and ask the children to complete all the sentences by selecting words from the board and writing them in the spaces provided.

Share the finished work within the group, reading back the sentences using voices appropriate to the words chosen.

Animal threats

Learning intentions
● to build awareness of features of character and dialogue
● to read text aloud with intonation and expression

Organization
● whole class

Re-read the whole story with the class. Discuss with the children the animals' behaviour towards Steven. What do they want from him and what tactics do they use in order to get what they want? Ask the children how they would feel if they were confronted like this. Discuss how Steven handles the situation. Is there any other action he could have taken? Draw attention to the fact that Steven outwits each of the animals.

Look at the pages where the monkey demands the bananas. Read it out using a calm voice for the monkey. Ask the class if they think this is how it should be read and invite them to re-read it using appropriate expression. Discuss how the stories can be brought to life by varying the tone and pace of your reading.

The animals speak

"I want those eggs," _____ the bear.

"Give me those bananas," _____ the monkey.

"Give me those apples you have in your basket," _____ the kangaroo.

"Give me the oranges you have in your basket," _____ the goat.

"Give me those doughnuts," _____ the pig.

"Give me those crisps," _____ the elephant.

Speech marks

Learning intentions
● to identify speech marks in reading, understand their purpose and use them in their own writing

Organization
● small group
● enlarged copy of photocopiable page 20
● copies of photocopiable page 21

Enlarge photocopiable page 20 which shows the monkey talking to Steven. Discuss the text with the children asking them to show you which parts of the text show when someone is talking. Using two different colour

highlighting pens invite the children to underline the words spoken by the monkey in one colour and those spoken by Steven in the other colour. Focus on the use of speech marks to demarcate the beginning and end of spoken text.

Give out copies of photocopiable page 21. Explain to the children that they are to transfer the words contained within the speech bubbles to sentences below each picture. The sentence should show what the animal said, who said it and the correct use of speech marks, eg, *"Me noisy!" said the monkey.* You may need to complete the first example together before allowing the children to complete their own sheets.

Lift-the-flap

Learning intentions
● to recall events from the story
● to reinforce their word- and sentence-level skills through reading known text in a different context

Organization
● small group
● enlarged copies of photocopiable page 22

Enlarge photocopiable page 22 onto A3 paper. Show the children how to cut and

fold the sheet to make two lift-the-flap strips. Read the threats made by the animals printed on each section of the strips. Can they remember which animal made each threat?

Give out enlarged copies of photocopiable page 22 and ask the children to make their own lift-the-flap strips, drawing and labelling the correct animal beneath each flap. They may need to refer to the book in order to match the sentences with the correct animals.

Speech marks (text)

 "Give me those bananas," said the monkey, "or I'll pull your hair."

 "If I threw a banana on to that kennel, you're so noisy I bet you couldn't get it without waking the dog."

"Me noisy!" said the monkey...

Speech marks (activity)

'I'll pull your hair.'

cut

'I will hug all the breath out of you.'

cut

'I'll squash you against the railings.'

fold

'I'll thump you.'

cut

'I'll whack you with my trunk.'

cut

'I'll butt you over the fence.'

fold

cut

Shopping Lists

Learning intentions
- to use simple word books to locate words by using the initial letter
- to use plurals appropriately

Organization
- small group
- copies of photocopiable page 24

Write out all the letters of the alphabet on small pieces of card. Lay these face down on the table. Ask one of the children to turn over one letter. Use a simple word book to find something that could be bought at the shop beginning with that letter.

Repeat this a few times until the children get the idea. Are there some letters for which it is harder to find a suitable item than others?

Give each child a copy of the blank shopping list on photocopiable page 24. Explain that they should each pick a letter and try to find something in the word book to add to their shopping list. As the items are numbered 1 to 6 remind them to use plurals where appropriate, *eg, 1 fish, 2 cakes, 3 sausages, etc.* The finished shopping lists could be illustrated.

Dear Animal

Learning intentions
- to respond personally to incidents in the story
- to write in response to what they have read

Organization
- whole class or small group

Discuss with the children how they feel about the animals' behaviour towards Steven. If they had the opportunity to talk to the animals what would they say? Encourage them to think about why bullying is wrong, how it makes the victim feel and the consequences it has for the perpetrator in terms of friendship and happiness.

Bearing the discussion in mind, the children should write a letter to one of the animals, encouraging them to stop their bullying behaviour. They should try to include persuasive arguments and offers of help.

Shopping list

1

2

3

4

5

6

Another shopping basket

Learning intentions
● to identify aspects of story structure
● to use planning sheets to draft story writing
● to use the story structure as a basis for their own story writing

Organization
● whole class or small group
● copies of photocopiable page 26

Invite the children to write their own version of the story. Discuss with the children what aspects of the original story could be changed, eg the main character, the type of shop visited, the items bought, the animals encountered on the way home, the threats made.

Show the children the story planner on photocopiable page 26. Go through the different options with the children sharing their ideas. Give out copies of the planning sheets and ask the children to brainstorm their own ideas, recording them on the sheets. They should then select from their initial ideas to create their own version of 'The Shopping Basket'.

I went shopping

Learning intentions
● to practise recall skills
● to listen and recall verbal information

Organization
● whole class

Sit the children in a circle. Explain that you are going to play a memory game called 'I went shopping'. Choose a child to start. They should say out loud 'I went shopping and I bought . . .' completing the sentence with their own choice of an item that may have been bought at the shop, eg, 'I went shopping and I bought a loaf of bread.' The next child in the circle repeats the sentence, including the item chosen by the first child and adding one of

their choice, eg, 'I went shopping and I bought a loaf of bread and some biscuits.' Continue in this way until the children find it too difficult to remember the sequence, then allow the next child to start again with a new shopping list.

Another shopping basket

'The Shopping Basket' Story Planner	
Main Character	Animals
Shop/Shopping	
Places passed	Threats

Steven's explanation

Learning intentions
- to respond in role to the story
- to distinguish between fantasy and reality

Organization
- whole class

Take on the role of Steven's mother. Indicate when you are in role by sitting on a particular chair or leaving the carpet area and returning to introduce yourself in role. Address the children as though they were Steven. Ask "How could it have taken so long to fetch the shopping?" and add "Don't try telling me any of your made-up stories about animals or monsters attacking you on the way!"
The children are then invited to take on the role of Steven and to come up with a more feasible explanation as to what happened to one or more of the missing items of shopping. The teacher-in-role should respond by either believing or dismissing the child's explanation.

Story props

Learning Intentions
- to encourage oral retelling of the story

Organization
- small group
- photocopiable page 28 enlarged and copied onto card

Give a small group of children photocopiable page 28 enlarged and copied onto card. Ask them to decorate the characters using colouring pencils, felt pens, paint or collage materials and to cut them out. The finished characters can be stuck onto short pieces of dowelling to make stick puppets. Allow the children to use the puppets to retell the story using the text or in their own words. They could also be made available in the listening corner with a copy of the book on tape, or the children could be invited to make their own tapes of the story.

Story props

Consequences

Learning intentions

● to consider the consequences of alternative sequences of events
● to relate aspects of the story to their own experience

Organization

● whole class

On a board or large sheet of paper draw three columns headed as below.

Recall how Steven dealt with the threats from the animals. Think again of other actions that Steven could have taken. Ask the children for suggestions of what Steven might have done and write these in the first column. For each action ask whether they think it would be a good or bad thing to do and what the consequence may be in terms of how Steven would feel and whether it would be a safe or wise course of action. Record these in the appropriate columns.

Ask the children if they can think of any examples where they have found themselves in a similar situation to Steven. Would any of the suggestions be useful to them in their own lives?

Steven could have . . .	Good Idea/Bad Idea	Consequence

USING THIS BOOK

The activities in this book are designed to help develop children's response to stories in the early stages of their literacy development. The emphasis is on text-level work, while many of the activities also provide opportunities for sentence- and word-level work.

The **Ways in** activity provides ideas for introducing the book to children. Opportunities are provided for considering basic text conventions, such as the title, author and blurb, and also for helping children to develop strategies for making critical choices in selecting their own reading materials by considering favourite authors and the use of the cover to provide clues as to the content of the story.

The **Making sense** whole-class activities allow the teacher to explore with the children ways in which meaning is communicated through the choice of vocabulary, the use of punctuation and aspects of story structure. The group activities provide opportunities for children to explore these ideas in greater depth.

The **Developing ideas** activities allow the children to explore the story in different ways: through playing games, creative writing and through art and music. They aim to develop personal responses and encourage children to revisit the book on many occasions,

feeling confident in their independent reading or retelling of the story.

The **Evaluation** activity encourages children to consider alternative strategies that Steven could have employed in tackling the animals. It tries to help children make links between the story and issues of bullying that they may encounter. By looking at the consequences of actions children are encouraged to think about their own behaviour and to take responsibility for the choices thay make in their own lives.

Classroom Management

The activities can be used across a number of literacy sessions. It is suggested that the book is introduced using the 'Ways In' activity, followed by the reading of the story as outlined on page 5. Further sessions could begin with a whole class activity, followed by groups of children working on related activities, differentiated to meet individual needs.

Access to multiple copies of the book will enhance the learning opportunities for many of the activities, though a number can also be successfully completed without direct access to the text.

Including a range of activities within a single literacy session – whole class, small group with adult support and group or individual activities that can be

The Shopping Basket

completed independently – will make the session more manageable and enable the teacher to target particular learning intentions with chosen groups of children.

Differentiation

The activities are intended to cover the range of literacy development throughout Key Stage 1. Activities should be selected to meet the needs of groups of children. A number of the activities, both whole class and group, can be differentiated by outcome and may therefore be suitable for children at all stages of literacy development. Providing opportunities for children to report back on their work at the end of each session will allow all children to experience a wide range of activities.

Linking Activities

The **Making Sense** activities include both whole class and group activities. In this book the four whole class activities are each followed by appropriate group activities which reinforce or extend similar learning intentions as shown in the following grid.

Matching the Book to your Class

John Burningham is a well established favourite among many primary school children. His books often follow a similar format which allows children to predict what may happen and to enjoy fully the

Activities	General learning intentions
Reading the story Steven's route Story structure What happened next? Story connections	• Knowledge of the story • Recalling information • Familiarisation with story structure – sequence, events, characters, settings
What did Steven buy? Give me that! Shopping basket game	• Word recognition • Hearing and identifying initial sounds in words
Sentence building The animals speak	• Using synonyms and other alternative words to change or enhance the meaning of a sentence
Animal threats Speech marks Lift-the-flap	• Looking at how direct speech is recorded in text

humour within both the text and the illustrations. 'The Shopping Basket' combines children's own experiences of going shopping with a fantasy world of talking animals and so is able to confront anxieties children may have of being bullied in a non-threatening manner.

The repetitive formula allows early readers to feel confident in retelling or re-reading the story while providing many opportunities for more established readers to extend their skills

Teaching Potential of 'The Shopping Basket'

The skills grid on the inside back cover outlines the areas of reading strategies, comprehension and response skills covered by the activities.

Opportunities are also available for other learning intentions, many of which fulfil the teaching requirements of the National Literacy Strategy, while others provide cross-curricular links.

Prior teaching/Background knowledge

Children will need to be familiar with the idea of returning to a book several times to explore different aspects of it. They will also need to be used to working in groups on different activities either independently, collaboratively or with an adult.

Recommended Classroom Resources

For all activities it is assumed that the children will have access to writing and drawing materials. In addition, many of the activities require access to general art materials and equipment, including glue, scissors, paints, and colouring pens and pencils. Specific resources for individual activities are listed under the 'Organization' heading.

Books Useful for Wider Reading
Books by John Burningham:
John Norman Patrick McHennessy, The Boy Who Was Always Late
Mr Gumpy's Outing
Mr Gumpy's Motor Car
Oi! Get Off Our Train
Where's Julius
Cannonball Simp
Time to get out of the bath, Shirley
Would You Rather ...
Avocado Baby
Granpa
Seasons
Harquin
ABC
Around the World in Eighty Days
Come away from the water, Shirley
Trubloff
Aldo
Borka
Humbert
Courtney

Picture Books (thematically linked):
Wait and See – Tony Bradman and Eileen Browne
On the Way Home – Jill Murphy
We're Going On A Bear Hunt – Michael Rosen
Handa's Surprise – Eileen Browne